My shattered self

My way out of depersonalisation and derealisation

by
V.M. Dame

©2020

Foreword

This book was written by me in the year of 2016.
I have translated it into English to reach more people
and help them with depersonalisation & derealisation.
This book is dedicated to all the people that are
suffering from this crippling condition.

I am not a doctor or psychologist.
This book was written to give you inspiration and
hope for your way out of the DP & DR.
This book is no replacement for a professional
treatment.
Please consult your doctor if you have severe medical
issues.

I was weak and I thought I was going insane.
My psyche was totally off.
I have experienced things, that are hard to put down in
words.
I was so deep in this weird and uncomfortable state
that I thought, I would never make it out.

But I did.
I am alive, happy and free of DP & DR
I want the same for you.
It takes a litle bit of strength and courage, but you will
also make it, no matter how long you have been

dealing with this state.

This book is translated, improved and thoughtfully re-written by me in May 2020.

Don't lose hope.
Hope is the fuel you will need for this journey.

For my dearest friends and family.
I would be lost without you.
You are my guiding light.

Contents

Hello you.
No, you are not crazy.
You are not going to lose it, no matter how hard you try.
You are not alone.
We are many.
You can rest in my arms now.
You can listen to my words now.
Let me help you.
I am with you right now.
I can feel you.
Let us share this pain.
We are many.
You are allowed to give yourself a break now.
A break from this terror inside of your head.
I am here with you.

1. At the beginning
1.1 My story

Hey there.
My name is Vanessa.
I am a quite normal, modern-day woman.
Is is a rainy day in May 2020.
I am 32 years old now.
I am sitting on my desk, while I am looking out of my window.
The sky is gray today. It rained a lot.
But the sun breaks through sometimes.
Very softly it shines with a gentle beam but the sun will break through the heavy clouds, I just know it.
It won't take long until there will be sunny days again.
They are lying ahead, just wating for us.
It's kind of funny how this reminds me of a time in my life in which I was not feeling very well.
A time, in which my head was full of clouds and rain.
And a time, in which I thought the sun will never rise up for me again.
I was afraid of the dark emptiness which I never thought would leave me again.
Yet I am here.
I have made it out of there.
And I am happy now.
When I watch any kind of sport on the TV, I am always cheering for the smaller teams.
The underdogs.

I like them because they really have to fight for their victory.
Like I did.
Now I am able to feel again.
To feel my own emotions.
I am able to laugh, to feel anger, pain, frustration, joy, love and hope.
I am fully back in control over my emotions.
I feel the whole palette of emotions.
This is nothing special for the majority of people.
They would never question this.
But there was a time in my life, where this was not given.
Where you would question your whole existence and your own being.
And I had never thought of writing the words I am writing today.
But here we are.
And this is my story.

It was back in September 2013.
Like for most of the people suffering from a dissociative disorder, mine was induced by drug abuse.
I mean nothing too crazy, okay?!
I just smoked a joint!
And... and I didn't do it all by myself.
It was on a party!
I did it with some of my friends back then.

I was 25 years old. .
Smoking weed was something that my body and mind never tolerated very well.
I was on some bad trips with dope, like being paranoid and stuff, and I got some severe panic attacks from it before.
This is why I never took the heavy stuff, I just knew, that I wouldn't be too much of a decent human being taking cocaine or LSD or something like that.
But I have never known that there was something like depersonalisation or derealisation, that you could get from just smoking weed.
I thought it was quite a harmless drug, even though I have made some bad experience with it.
I thought so many times:
„Why couldn't you let it be this one time, girl?"
I felt so guilty for smoking this joint with my friends.
But I didn't know what would happen to me back then, right?
I didn't know, that my life would turn upside down a few minutes after I've had inhaled the sweet vapor of the weed.
That constant finger pointing at my own self didn't help much *healing* from the dissociative disorder.
(Note from the author: Please keep in mind that I use the word healing not in the sense of healing from a injury or real disease or illness. I still use this word as it feels like healing for many people affected by DPDR.)

But first things first:
Please, don't get me wrong here.
It's true, I didn't do drugs on a regular basis.
I was more somewhat of a drinker and sometimes I
smoked a joint with my friends if one of them had
dope to share.
But it doesn't matter if you have this condition due to
regular drug use, semi-regular drug use, occasional
drug use or no drug use at all.
There is the same chance.
There is a way back for everyone.

Back to my story.
I was thriving at this time of my life.
I was young and just started college to become a
veterinary technician.
I was very fit, I exercised a lot and started to change
my nutrition to become a healthier person.
Enjoying my youth, I went out drinking once in a
while and hanging out with my friends or going
dancing at some clubs downtown.
After I took the second puff of the joint that night, I
started feeling funny.
At first, I tried to ignore that feeling and I tried to
particape in the conversation with that laid-back
atmosphere that the rest of the group had.
But from this moment on, there was just something
different about me.
Something was off but I couldn't really point my

finger at it.
It was like the reality was not real anymore.
The little party went on and I just waited for this feeling to be over or the drug to lose its effect, but neither happened.
Everything felt kind of dull and disconnected.
I was thinking about this situation all of the time and suddenly, I got a severe panic attack, I couldn't breathe and I began to cry.
One of my friends grabbed my hand and took me out of the house to the garden.
She was able to calm me down.
I talked to her and told her everything, as I was scared in that moment.
She did not understand what I was talking about but she was very calming and promised me, that everything was going to be okay on the next day.
Her words helped me and I just tried to ignore this feeling and went to bed, becaue I wanted to believe her.
Everything was going to be okay the next day, except it wasn't.
I was so exhausted from this whole experience that I fell asleep within minutes.

The next day came and I went to class.
Something I had known, a daily routine that was familiar.
But still – there was something off.

This dull feeling, the feeling to be disconnected from the outside world was persistent.
I used to be a very good student who loved being in class and taking notes of everything.
Unable to focus, I made the decision to take my phone to the ladie's washroom and started to insert a description of my symptons into a search engine.
I was overwhelmed by the result of the search and this was the beginning of the end.

„Schizophrenia – Help! I am going crazy!"

„Funny feeling after smoking weed doesn't go away. What can I do? I have been having this for over 5 years now!"

„I am suffering from these symptoms for over 25 years. You will never get rid of them."

„You shouldn't have been smoking weed anyway! Some people get what they deserve."

„That's a psychosis probably. You should get some help or admit yourself to a mental hospital right now."

It was time for the next panic attack, my hands sweating, I was shaking.
All alone in the washroom with these weird symptoms and all those threads written on the internet.

I think, I have never felt more alone in my entire life.
I was paralyzed and in a state of shock.
The refreshing energy of cold water on my face from
the tap helped me to get out of this state and I made
my way back to class.
I tried to not think about all the stuff on the internet
but I just couldn't, all of my thoughts just revolved
around this topic.
Maybe my physical appearance was in that classroom,
but my mind surely wasn't.

„Will it be like this forever?"
„Who am I?"
„What's going on, why do I feel like surreal?"
„It's my own fault. I deserve this."
„What if this never stops?"

I was spending the evening in my dorm room reading
everything I could find about this „condition" on the
internet.
All of them were horror stories, there was no
exception.
Not a single positive post about this feeling I could
find.
I lied to my college friends and told them I was
feeling sick.
I didn't want to participate in any social event.
I wanted to be alone and that's what I did, together
with all of these stories.

I consumed them and I was shocked by the sheer amount of negativity regarding this topic.
I cannot remember how, but I must have fallen asleep while reading those stories.
The next day started out even worse.
When I woke up, I felt like I was living inside of a bubble or a dome made of glass.
I couldn't feel myself anymore.
I was totally disconnected from myself and from the outside world.
It was like there was a invisible barrier between me and everything else.
I went to the friend who brought the marihuana along and he told me that everything was fine with the weed.
With hesitance I told him a little bit about my funny condition.
He had said that he thought, that I was suffering from a psychosis.
I got nervous.
I have never had a psychosis before, so I wouldn't know how it worked.
I did suffer from depression before but I didn't know much about psychological issues back then.
Back to the ladie's washroom, where I got my third panic attack in two days.
It would have been better for me to know what a psychosis was.
If I would have known, I would have not been so

afraid of it, like I was.

I was even afraid to look for the symptoms on the internet.

Too afraid the symptoms overlapping with mine.

If you have a psychosis, you are not able to ask yourself if you have a psychosis, because you just have it.

But at this point of my life, I was not aware of this and so I thought, my mental health was a mess and that I fucked up my life.

The following weeks and months were very dreadful.

Just right before all of this happened, I have met my former boyfriend and I felt so pressured because I wanted to be funny and open-minded, just the way he had met me.

I was in love (I couldn't feel it anymore due to the *bubble* I was living in, but I remember loving him a few days before), I wanted to be happy and I wanted to just enjoy ourselves as a young couple being in love, but I the truth was, I was devastated.

We had hardly known each other and I didn't want to tell him what was really going on with me.

If he had noticed, I was acting a bit off, I just told him that I had stress to deal with.

It was a charade and despite trying to pretend I was fine and that I was actually feeling any kind of emotions which I didn't and studying to get good grades I was also working part-time at a veterinary

clinic.
You can imagine that it didn't take long until this house of cards came falling down.
I confessed everything to my now ex-boyfriend.
I told him about the anxiety, panic attacks, of the feeling I was living underneath a dome or inside of a bubble, that I could not feel myself, that I felt the world was surreal, that I alienated from everything that I thought was normal and that I felt like a stranger in my own body.
And for a moment I really thought:
„That's it! That dude's gonna leave me for sure. Farewell my lover."
But to my big surprise he just hugged me and confessed to me, that he had been going through the same symptoms a few years back.
That he was still suffering from panic and anxiety attacks and that he also had felt the dissociation before.
He reassured me that everything was going to be okay and that, despite from his rare attacks, he was fine again.
It was such a huge relief.
He gave me some advice and told me to seek out a psychologist to talk about the issues.

A few days later I did see a psychologist and it was very good thing talking to her.
She could calm me down a little bit and tried to

educate me on different topics, e.g. how a psychosis works and we started talking about my immediate past and some things that happened long before.

The feeling of living underneath a dome made of glass began to decrease and at first I thought, I finally made some positive progress.

But the true horror was just about to begin.

The next months of my life were filled with anxiety, horror, panic, depression, fears, intrusive thoughts, alienation from everything and everyone I have loved, alienation from my own emotions that became even worse, derealisation, etc.

And now?

Now I am happy and free from all of this.

Of course I am prone to depression but it is no comparison to everything what happened back then.

Happily all of this are just memories now.

I am free again.

I feel alive again.

I am happy again.

And I was in a very deep dissociative state of mind.

With this book I want to help you out of this condition as we take it step by step.

I want to give you hope and trust in the process.

Before we start, let's try to settle a few things first.

1. Try to make yourself as comfortable as possible.

I know it is hard when you just have those strange feelings and intrusive thoughts and a high anxiety-level like 24/7.
But maybe you can try to start the healing-process like this:
Reading this book with a cup of tea is your safe space in your day.
You are not allowing intrusive thoughts and anxiety to invade this safe space.
It will take some practice but it will be very helpful.

2. The most important thing and a immediate step you can take to heal, is to quit searching the internet for your symptoms.
The times might have changed a bit.
I know that there is more positive information about derealisation and depersonalisation now, but still there is a lot of bad things and false information written about this topic.
It is best to stop this behaviour as it is very toxic and can worsen your current state.
If you are trying to stop it and you have setback, forgive yourself and try to start again.
Little steps are the key to success.

3. Being negative towards yourself and feeling guilty is toxic for your journey to recovery.
It would be great if you could find something, you really like about yourself.

It could be your talent for playing the guitar, having nice legs, cooking skills or something else.
The more positive aspects you can find about yourself, the better!
It could feel weird in the beginning though, as you could have lost your sense for yourself.
When you are very deep in this state like me it also can be weird beause you don't feel your existense at all.
I know the feeling of positivity can be scary during deperonalisation and derealisation, but try to get used to it, step by step, day by day.
Being nice and forgiving to yourself is very important.

4. I will use the abbreviation *DPDR* for depersonalisaton and derealisation.
In the end both of these disorders are similar and have the same mechanism but the symptoms are a little bit different.
This book is for depersonalisation AND derealisation.
I had to deal with both of these conditions, one being stronger as the other from time to time.

5 Get yourself used to the fact that there is no immediate solution.
Unfortunately there is no pill that does magic wonders and make the DPDR go away.
The recovery process *is a process* indeed, with all ups and downs and setbacks.

It could take you weeks, months or even years.
But no matter how long, you will make it out of this
condition and with reading this book you already
made the first step.
And it's worth all of the struggle.
I'd rather go through this recovery process one million
times than to ever feel the DPDR again.

This book may also contain triggers.
Sometimes I have to be very blunt about certain
topics.
Also we could trigger some past trauma, irrational
fears and intrusive thoughts.
Take this book step by step as well and if you don't
feel that you have enough strength for this journey,
just leave it to another day.
It is so important that you treat yourself very kindly
and that you give yourself time.

Note that the DPDR is never present 24/7.
I know it feels like it, but the truth is, it's not.
There are moments during the day where you don't
have the DPDR, you are just not aware of this beause
you are lost in thoughts, etc.
As soon as you will start with the recovery process,
you will feel DPDR-free moments throughout your
day.
You can get excited about this and suddenly you will
think of the DPDR agian and it will be back indeed.

This is very normal during the recovery.
In the beginning you will start to notice those moments, later on you will not.
It will be like one hour free from DPDR and after the hour you start to think:
„Hey where did the DPDR go?" and then you will have it again.
This is the normal recovery process.
If you start to feel this, congrats you are on the right track!
Nonetheless there are already DPDR-free moments in your life right now.
You are just not realising them.
Also there is times when the symptoms are worse and when they are better.
The constant level of a 24/7 DPDR is a myth.
I thought the same but it turned out to be untrue.

I am ready when you are!
Shall we get started then?

1.2 What is a dissociative disorder?

I think most of you already know what the description
of a dissociative disorder is.
It means that everything which is connected
instinctively from the psychological aspect, suddendly
feels disconnected and strange.
All of your memories, your identity, your personality
traits, friends, family, objects, the world, the universe
and yes, even being a human can feel alien and
wrong.
The dissociative disorder comes in many forms but
they share the same mechanism most of the time.

*Why is a dissociative disorder happening in the first
place?*

There is still so much scientific research to be done.
My own research and most of the scientific evidence
say, that dissociative disorders happen as a natural
defense mechanism against current or past traumatic
situations, which are hard to process or hurt
emotionally.

Is a dissociative disorder dangerous?

I get this question a lot beause it feels dangerous,
indeed.
But no, it is not dangerous or harmful in any kind of

way!

When you are in this state of mind it is really hard to believe this, but it functions as a *natural defense mechanism* und leaves no harm whatsoever.

In contrary to *how* it feels, the depersonalisation and the derealsation are a sign of a well working psyche.

Especially empathetic and sensitive people suffer from DPDR.

Unfortunately there are many people who suffer from psychosis, schizophrenia or other dissociative disorders.

If you would have a mental illness, you'd probably have on of these.

The DPDR feels like one but in fact it wants to keep you sane.

And you having this condition instead of one of the other mental illnesses, shows that your defense mechanism is working and that your psychological health is granted.

I am aware that it does not *feel* like it.

But as we proceed with this book I am sure you will understand how this defense mechanism works.

Everything is totally fine with you.

You just need a little push in the right direction.

Also it is important to know, that no matter how long you have been suffering from DPDR, you can always recover from it.

Everyone can get out of this condition.

It may be a little bit harder for people who have been

suffering 10 years plus from it, because the longer you have it, the more resistant it will be.

That means people suffering from it 10 years plus will have to work a little bit harder on it, but in the end everyone can get rid of the DPDR.

It is a scary feeling when your perception starts tov shift back to your „old" and „normal" reality.

When this happened to me, I started to run back and hide behind the DPDR in the beginning..

This is why it needs little steps to get used to the old normal.

If you are so used to your new perception, like suffering from it 10 years plus, it is more than understandable that recovery might take a little bit longer.

So taking a step outside of your shield can be scary and what happens next?

Your defense mechanism is on high alert again and the DPDR kicks back in heavily.

All in all, it is important to understand, that it does not matter how long you have been suffering from DPDR.

Being brave and believing in yourself is what matters.

Getting help from this book to find the right direction and taking the right steps is important.

I know this condition makes it so hard to believe that you can come out of it.

It makes you feel helpess and hopeless.

But I am the living proof speaking to you right now,

that you are able to defeat the DPDR.
And even if you are not convinced, it doesn't harm you in any way to try it out and find your way back to your old perception.
You have nothing to lose but a lot to win (back).

1.3 Common symptoms and triggers

This chapter is talking about many symptoms which could be a trigger for some readers.
Please just proceed reading if you are feeling stable enough.

The dissociative disorder is very multifaceted.
But why do I still call it disorder, when in the last chapter I talked about it as a natural defense mechanism?
Well, good question!
The DPDR itself is a natural defense mechanism, reacting to a high level of emotional stress and / or anxiety and / or trauma.
It actually is a reaction to protect our mind from further damage, like schizophrenia, etc.
Every single person experiences DPDR in one way or another during their lifetime.
The DPDR also happens with animals, but we are going to discuss that in another chapter.
This condition being chronic though, is a malfunction that needs a little bit of help to go away.
So I wouldn't call it a disorder like schizophrenia or a psychosis, which also belong to the dissociative disorders.
But they all do share the same kind of mechanism.
So I use this word „dissociative disorder", even if I do not see the DPDR as an actual disorder.

The setlist of symptoms varies for each individual. There are many different symptons and one seems to be even more „crazy" than the other. It seems that no one shares the same setlist oft symptons, as it can vary according to what triggers the most anxiety at the moment.

Definition and symptons of depersonalisation:
Depersonalisation is feeling a disturbance in the sense of your own self.

Symptoms *can* be:

- feeling like life is a dream / thinking that life is just a dream
- issues with the perception of the own self
- out-of-body-experience
- feeling like a robot / thinking you are a robot
- seeing yourself / seeing yourself from the bird's eye view
- recognition of the own self in the mirror / on photographs is not possible
- alienation from own voice
- not being capable of feeling any emotions / feeling cut off from own emotions
- the feeling to lose control or to go „crazy"
- feeling inhuman (like a zombie / demon etc.)

Definition and symptoms of derealisation:
Derealisation is feeling cut off from the outside world and a disturbance in the perception and the experience of the outside world and reality.

Symptons *can* be:

- impaired vision
- visual snow / incapable of recognizing colors
- feeling surreal / feeling „not here"
- the world and the life feels like if they are a movie and not a real experience
- feeling like living inside of a bubble / dome / nutshell
- disturbance in the sense of time / not able to recognize seasons
- feeling cut off from own memories / memories feel alien
- objects feel alien
- other humans feel surreal / like a zombie / like a demon / like a robot etc.

On top of all of this weird symptoms, most people also suffer from:

- anxiety
- panic attacks
- insomnia
- intrusive thoughts

- suicidal thoughts
- anxiety attacks
- depression
- feeling anorectic

And especially **irrational fears** are playing a huge part regarding the DPDR.
We will also talk about this in particular in another chapter.

I was asked quite frequently if depersonalisation and derealisation are different.
But they aren't. The only difference is the symptons.
There are people who are affected more by depersonalisation, others are more affected by derealisation.
Most of the time you are suffering from a combination of both of them, like me.
They are the same, it just depends on which of them gives you the most anxiety.
My symptoms included:

- living inside of a bubble
- feeling like a stranger to myself
- cut off from my own emotions
- issues with the first person perspective
- depression
- anorexia
- insomnia

- panic attacks
- the outside world felt alien
- philosophical questions about our existence, which would keep me up all night
- irrational fears
- anxiety attacks
- the feeling to live outside of my body
- the feeling to be just made out of eyes, like my body would not exist anymore
- my body felt strange, like looking at my hands and other body parts scared me
- memory loss
- I wasn't able to focus on anything anymore
- brain fog

The symptoms changed all of the time in my case. Maybe I have had one, then another one came, a third one joined, the first one disappeared but came back a few monhts later and so on.
It took some time until I finally realized that there was a pattern behind it.
If one symptom didn't induce enough anxiety to keep the DPDR going, there would be another one to take its place to frighten the hell out of me.
Intrusive thoughts as well as anxiety and panic attacks were part of my everyday life back then.
I was living my whole life in fear.

Triggers and reasons for DPDR

It took me a while to understand that the joint was not the reason for this condition.
I felt guilty for so many months, my mum always warned me about using drugs and I couldn't take the pressure of the guilt anymore.
I really hope that you are not like me.
If you took any drugs, don't blame yourself.
It is a good time to think about drug usage, but the shame and guilt has to stop in order to heal from the DPDR.
The reason for it lies somewhere else.
My psychologist was able to help me with this issue.
She explained a lot to me and I figured out why all of this happened to me.
The joint was a trigger, not the reason.
There could be any reason, though!
Energy-drinks, coffee, painkillers, a stressful situation and sometimes it seems that it can even rise out of nowhere.
But in most cases the DPDR is induced by a drug.
It is also not relevant if you have used the drug many times before or if it was the first time.

Like I have already mentioned earlier, it seems that most of the affected are very sensitive and empathetic human beings.
They also seem to have a hard time to get a proper

distance from the negative feelings and thoughts of their fellow human beings surrounding them.

Most of the affected are reporting that they have issues with setting boundaries or even are a people pleaser.

They often get used from other people to listen to their problems without getting anything in return or not even asking for anything in return.

It seems like the roots for getting DPDR can be found in the childhood.

Maybe you can start thinking about someone who acts like that.

It could be your parents, your partner, your sister, your boss or a friend.

It is very important to set healthy boundaries with this person / or persons in the future.

It seems like I am just saying it like that.

This is easier said than done, right?

I know it myself.

It was hard for me to realize how many people were harming me with their behaviour.

The most toxic person in my life,I've had to cut out, was my own father because he is a narcissist.

It is not meant like you have to cut out everyone now, who doesn't make you feel good.

Dealing with people who are difficult is part of our life.

But there are cases where it is the best option.

After I have realized that my father is a narcissist, I

still tried to deal with him and set boundaries for myself.

It was when he wanted me to do something totally out of my plans, that he told me that I would not be his daughter anymore if I did not do what he wanted me to, that I made the decision to cut him out.

It was the last time that I have tried to deal with him.

Of course I did not do what he wanted me to do and proceeded with my life according to my own plans.

He then abandoned me and up til now, I am very happy with this situation.

It took me a few therapy sessions but I am okay with it now.

My life is better without him and I felt guilty in the beginning.

But I have learnt that I cannot live my life according to his wishes and the guilt-tripping just had to stop.

If he ever wants to be in touch with me again, I will not decline him, but I will be careful.

This is just one example and it is an extreme one.

For you it doesn't have to be like this.

It could be that you just have to step back a little from a connection or show them your new boundaries.

If people really love you, they will accept them.

Give people around you some time to get used to your new boundaries, but eventually they are going to love you either way.

This is my experience.

And this is not something you can do overnight.

It takes training and discipline to live by your new boundaries.

People will try to bend and push them, because they don't know you in a different way.

Also it is the time now that you just take care of yourself.

Some of you could have a lot of obligations regarding the family.

If you are not feeling well it is totally fine to take some time off.

Not everyone can rely on you.

Of course sometimes you cannot break out of these obligations totally, but then try to make the most time for yourself as possible.

I've had the same issues with my family.

Not only is my father a narcissist, the whole family dynamic from my father's side was toxic.

My grandparents had put expectations on me and when I did not want to live up to those, I was the black sheep of the family.

Guilt and shame have always been a great part of my life and it took me quite some time to see beyond these patterns.

My life has a better quality right now.

I don't have to deal with this side of the family anymore.

They have always been critisizing me for the way I live, just because I did not want to be like the rest of the family and I wanted to experience something else, something more than the life they wanted me to have.

There are some other reasons for the DPDR:

- a high / extreme level of anxiety and fear
- a high / extreme level of stress
- burnout
- trauma
- obsessive compulsive disorder
- depression (you can have DPDR because of depression, or depression because of DPDR)
- side effects of drugs / medicine
- PTSD
- anxiety disorder
- epilepsy
- borderline personality disorder

So we have to make a difference between the trigger and the reason(s) for the DPDR.
The DPDR was already inside of you, the pill, drug, joint, drink etc., was just the trigger.
The tip of the iceberg.

I have talked to many people affected by DPDR and most of those who have come out of this condition, found the root for it in their past.
In a later chapter we will talk more about the root cause analysis and how you best prepare for it and to proceed with it.

But for now, I want to talk about the most frequently asked question, regarding DPDR.

1.4 Am I going insane?

„I am going insane, oh god please help!"
„I'm gonna lose it!"
„I have a psychosis."
„Help me, I am going mad!"

I am sure that these questions are or were inside of your head and there is / was no end to it.
During my recovery process there was a time, when I even got annoyed by this question.
My brain would just continue with this topic.
Endless loops of the same questions over and over and over.
And it didn't happen.
I have never lost it.
This is probably the most frequently asked question when it comes to DPDR.
And the answer is: No.
No, **you are *not going crazy*** and ***you are not crazy.***
I promise you that.
„How does she know?", you might ask.
And I will answer you this question.
As we have seen before, the DPDR is a very normal defense mechanism, that is just a little malfunctioned and this feels really ugly.
The DPDR is based on the *fight-and-flight-syndrome* and also animals have this.
If a gnu is facing a lion, it literally has two options:

Either it is going to fight the lion, or it is going to run away.
This mechanism always takes place when there is great danger or a traumatic event a living being has to face.
Great danger and trauma means high adrenaline levels, fear and anxiety and can lead to dissociaton in order to survive.
The only thing that is different from a passing dissociation condition is, that the one you are dealing with right now became chronic.
Unfortunately this thing happens and it is horrible and the science didn't really put much effort into researching this topic.
There are a few explanations now and all of them are based on the fight-or-flight-syndrome.
Due to anxiety and other psychological reasons this natural phenomenon can become a problem.
Something that was made to safe us, suddenly is something that is so crippling and frustrating.
And this DPDR needs one thing to stay chronic: Anxiety and fear.

DPDR is not a progressive condition, it will not leave any physical damage on your brain whatsoever.
The same goes for the psychological aspect.
There is no damage at all.
When you made it out of the DPDR, it is just like it was before the time when you got this condition.

When you are *healed,* most people cannot even remember how it felt.
I had a very severe case of DPDR, so I still can remember the horror and the anxiety.
But it does not bother me anymore, because I am out of it and most of the thoughts I had, don't make sense anymore.
I really want to emphasize that there is no harm you have to fear.
It doesn't matter how long you have been suffering from this condition.
It will pass and everything will be fine again.
It will not change your personality in a negative way.
The DPDR can only make you stronger and more sensitive and it can give you another, more thoughtful perception of life.
The DPDR will soon just be one chapter in the long story called your life.
The DPDR cannot lead to another mental illness.
The DPDR is a sign that your mental health works just fine.
It is only the malfunction that transformed it into a chronic condition, due to anxiety and / or stress or other reasons, which we have discussed and you are not able to shake off.
So the DPDR is a proof that you are mentally stable.
It is just that you are probably a bit sensitive and maybe you need to set new boundaries and reduce anxiety and stress.

So therefor the DPDR is not a pre-state of a another mental illness.
The DPDR *can* be a comorbidity of the following, mental illnesses:

- Schizophrenia
- Multiple personality disorder
- Borderline personality disorder
- Psychosis
- Obsessive compulsive disorder
- Depression
- other personality disorders

So the DPDR alone can be a condition (and in addition other conditions can appear, like depression etc.), that is what you have, or it can occur as a additional condition with one of the disorders stated above.
Through my thorough research and interviews with people affected by personality disorders as stated above, I have found out that in these cases the DPDR is just a passing episode.
They have an intense feeling of the DPDR, but they usually snap out of it quite fast.

I don't want to make you feeling uncomfortable now.
I am sure that you do not have schizophrenia, multiple personality disorder and a psychosis.
„Why?", you might ask.

Because if you would have one of these conditions, you wouldn't ask yourself if you've had them.
If you've had a psychosis you could maybe believe that you'd be a fairy and living in the woods.
There would be no question for you if this was real or you wouldn't be scared if you've had a psychosis or schizophrenia, etc. because it would just be your new reality.
You would not question yourself.
DPDR *feels* wrong but there is actually nothing wrong with you.

The exception here is borderline personality disorder and the obsessive compulsive disorder.
With those disorders you usually do not create an alternate reality which you believe is the truth.
If you have the suspicion that you might suffer from one of these conditions, it would be the best option to talk to your doctor and a professional person about this.
But there is a lot more to it than just DPDR.
So don't be afraid now of these disorders and illnesses.
They are very well researched in science and there is a very good treatment available.

The same goes for schizophrenia, MP and a psychosis.
Due to connections, I could initiate a interview with a doctor from a mental hospital in my hometown.

There are a lot of people with these conditions and the treatment, research and medical help is very advanced in this field.
These conditions are retrogressive and even if you've had one of them, you could go back to normal.

But as I've already said (and I do want to emphasize it again), as long as you are scared of being psychotic or have schizophrenia etc., you are not.
This is impossible.
You are not going to be mentally ill, because your defense mechanism worked and it worked a little too well.

If you are like me, maybe these thoughts are running through your head right now:
„Maybe I am going to lose the fear of having a psychosis right now and then it will happen." or similar thoughts.
This is a game of your mind to keep the anxiety level high.
As long as you are scared of getting these conditions or as long as you are afraid of stopping to be afraid, everything is fine.
(Phew, those mindgames are really tough!)

2. The demystification
2.1 The daily routine – fear

I know that most of the people suffering from the
DPDR condition are having a hard time in trusting
something in general.
There is a lot written about the DPDR on the internet.
When you finally find someone who has *healed* from
this condition, the entry usually is quite short or
something like:
„It just went away after seven weeks."
„I tried acupuncture and it was gone.
„My doctor gave me xxx and it helped."
And you find yourself thinking
„Why isn't this working for me? Why can't it just be
gone?"
Maybe you started praying again, begging God to free
you from this horror.
Maybe you lost all hope.
Maybe sometimes you catch yourself staring at
random people, seeing them laughing and having a
good time.
And you get so jealous.
And maybe you get scared.
Because to you they suddenly start looking like
zombies, robots or demons.
Sometimes you just see them as a piece of flesh
without a soul, just blood, vessels and atoms.
And it scares you.

If you could only talk to somebody about what you are going through.

But you can't, because they'd think you are crazy, right?

And then the fear comes back that you really could be crazy.

Damn, you suddenly feel the urge to check the internet again, if it really does not make you insane.

And out of all the hundreds and hundreds of entries, you will find that one entry, where someone knows somebody who did have DPDR and was admitted with a psychosis to a mental hospital.

And you will just focus on this single entry.

Maybe you start thinking about what would happen if you'd need to be admitted to a mental hospital.

Would you lose your job?

What would your friends and family say?

What about your reputation?

Would you ever get out of there again or would it finally destroy you completely?

All those meds, tranquilizers and maybe a straightjacket.

It sounds like a nightmare.

And the circle of fear begins again.

This was a typical thought pattern of a day in my life with DPDR.

Do you have similar thoughts and patterns?

At the peak of my time with DPDR, I was literally afraid of anything and anybody.

At the beginning of my story, I was living inside the infamous „bubble".
Everything felt kind of dull and nothing could really reach or touch me.
My voice was strange, the face inside the mirror was alien and I just felt so empty.
After my first two sessions with my psychologist the bubble did burst.
That was the time when the panic and anxiety really started to hit me.
My everyday life was draining, stressful and unsettling.
The day started with me waking up.
These were the most beautiful 10 to 15 seconds of the day.
The little moment between waking up and being back to full consciousness again.
That little slip between the sleep and the reality is what I enjoyed most.
Then my conscious kicked in and the DPDR was there, ready to ruin my day again.
I needed to get up early for veterinary college and it was very exhausting because I was suffering from sleeping issues and insomnia.
I felt tired constanly. There was no energy left.
The next horror waited for me in the bathroom:
Brushing my teeth, washing my face / or taking a shower, putting on some light make up.
(By the way, taking care of yourself is a important

step in healing from DPDR but we will get to it later!)
This was a challenge because I was so afraid of my
own reflection in the mirror, that I could just look at
myself for like 10 seconds.
Everything seemed just to be so weird.
My eyes, my mouth, my skin.
Nothing made sense anymore.
I tried to cope with it and finnished my morning
routine.
Sometimes I was so weak and tired I could not do it.
I would just brush my teeth, put on some deodorant,
avoiding my reflection in the mirror and leave the
house without doing my hair or washing myself.
The next challenge was taking the bus to college or to
my part-time job.
I've known my fellow commuters and the route.
But everything and everyone scared me.
I was always afraid of losing control in public.
That made things like shopping, meeting friends for a
coffee or going out almost impossible.
The cinema was the absolute worst challenge for me, I
remember that clearly.
I could not go.
It was too hard.

When I arrived at collge or work, I just ignored the
staring from the other people.
They could just tell that something was off with me.
I wasn't the funny, outgoing, gleaming, young woman

anymore.

She was gone.

I became this silent, sad, scared, sullen and depressed girl, who always seemed to be „not there".

I always tried to conceal what was going on inside of me.

I was sure that they couldn't undestand this.

I could not understand it myself.

I was also afraid, that people around me could call someone to pick me up and bring me into a mental hospital.

By the way, in the four years between the first edition of this book and the second edition now, I have admitted myself into a mental hospital.

Not because of DPDR, it was due to depression.

And it was not that bad!

I actually really liked it there.

But there will be a chapter about this topic later.

In the past, this was one of my biggest fears – the mental hospital.

Most of the time I could not smile anymore.

It was literally not possible.

Sometimes I just felt like a piece of flesh, sitting on a chair.

I was the complete opposite of how people used to know me.

My best friends were concerned and of course I kind of tried to tell them what was going on with me.

But this task was impossible.

It was very nice to see my friends trying really hard to understand me, it was nice to see how much they cared.
But they just couldn't understand it.
I just told most of the people that I was suffering from depression, which was not a lie but just half of the truth.
But it was more relatable and people would stop asking me questions, I did not want to answer or was just not able to answer.

When there was a night in which I could sleep for a few hours, I had the energy to actually participate in a conversation with my coworkers or fellow students.
The worried faces around me weren't making things any better.
The unspoken pity and people mourning my „old" personality, which seemed to be dead, pressured me the utmost.
„I MUST get out of this shit.", I remember thinking a lot.

During classes and work my ability to focus was not given.
Grades fell, my boss was not too happy with my performance.
I was scared of my colleagues, because I was afraid they could be posessed by a demon.
During class I was asking myself about my existence.

About the universe.
Those questions you don't have a answers to.
And they scared me.
I could barely eat anything.
In fact I was afraid of food.
Afraid of eating.
Afraid of digesting.
People were talking behind my back, saying I was
anorexic.
I kind of was anorexic, but because I was afraid of
eating food.
I could just think about of what food was made of and
that it was just atoms I put into atoms.
When I was sitting on a bench trying to take a break,
there was always the need to run away after a while.
I just wanted to run.
I could not relax and enjoy a moment of peace for
myself.

The situation didn't get any better at home.
I couldn't tell my room mates about this situation.
„Depression" was the reason for my appearance.
My ex-boyfriend was the only one I trusted with this
topic.
As I said, he had to deal with this too a few years
before, we have met when he was completely healed.
His condition was different though, but in the end it
was the same mechanism.
He would study in another city and during the week

we could just talk on the phone.
The calls were all about my fears and anxiety.
Day after day, week after week.
There was hardly anything else we could talk about.
The pressure to not fuck my relationship up did weigh heavy on my shoulders.
I felt so guilty all of the time, because it was all about me.
I didn't want that, but on the other side, I couldn't help it.
He was very understanding and even though we are not a couple anymore (not due to DPDR, we have had a „normal" relationship for a few years after my recovery), I will always be thankful for what he did for me.
Sometimes we were fighting because of my doubts.
He was the living proof that you could get out of this, but when my anxiety level was high, I did not believe him and could not trust the process.
So he ran out of patience once in a while and I am able to understand him, now and then.
Sometimes I got jealous because he had made it and I was still dealing with this shit.
I was like a little child and arrogant to not believe him.
„I know you made it, but my story is different! I will never make it. Your situation was way easier."
Those were some of the things I said when I was frustrated and couldn't go on anymore.

I threw the phone against my wall.
And it was true.
His condition wasn't that severe, but still he had been through the experience.

After the phone calls I usually tried to eat something.
I didn't want to eat but my body forced me by the end of the day.
I tried to go to bed and that was the time of the day when I started to dismantle my whole existence in my mind.
The thoughts were running wild.
Sometimes I got anxiety attacks that would have a physical effect on me.
I started shaking and I felt cold.
Sometimes I didn't sleep at all, sometimes it just happened naturally due to the exhaustion.

This was my everyday life with the DPDR.
When I think about it now, it makes me sad how I could let the fear consume me like that
But I didn't know it any better.
My world turned upside down.
The fear dictated me when to sleep or how I was sleeping, how much I ate, my relationships and my performance at college and work.
It destroyed everything.
Most of the people surrounding me gave me all the patience and understanding they could offer.

But I was pushing far beyond that.

This constant fear is what keeps the chronic DPDR
going.
Let's start dismantling this asshole together!

2.2 The flight-or-fight-syndrome

During my research regarding the DPDR, I have always been confronted with the flight-or-fight-syndrome.
I did not pay much attention to this biological topic, because I thought that this easy and natural explanation could not be part of the reason for this scary phenomenon inside of my head.
But also due to my studies at the veterinary college, I learnt more and more about hormones, biological process and how this could have a psychological effect on the brain.
So the flight-and-fight-syndrome came back to my mind and I finally could understand the connection between DPDR and this syndrome.
As I have stated many times before, the DPDR is a natural defnese mechanism.
I was asking myself quite often, from what excactly *this stupid thing* is saving me?
I was a open-minded, jolly, young woman, who've just happened to have a bit too much of potent weed.
Was there something else in my mind I forgot about?

What the heck happened that night back in 2013?

Our autonomic nervous system works on its own, automatic functions in our body are controlled by it, e.g. breathing, digestion, hormones, blood pressure etc.

There is no way you can really control it with your mind, there are things controlled by it you are not really aware of.

There is the *sympathetic* nervous system and the *parasympathetic* nervous system working for the autonomic nervous system.

The flight-and-fight-syndrome is an extremely rapid reaction to a danger you are facing in that moment.

There is no time pondering about a decision to make, when you are facing a lion that wants to have you for dinner.

So the body has this automatic response to a severe threat, when you have to decide how to survive in a blink of an eye.

Animals have that fight-or-flight-syndrome just as humans have it.

We still own this from our ancestors living in a cave, facing many deadly animals and dangers outside in the harsh world.

This happens automatically with the help of hormones (adrenaline) produced by the adrenal glands.

So what happens if you have a panic attack that feels sincerely live threatening, like me?

What happens if you feel like you are trapped in a situation that seems to be a threat?

What happens if there is a lot of stress going on in your mind and threatening your well-being?

Yes, the flight-or-fight-syndrome kicks in, wanting to

rescue you from a threat, that might be harmful for your psyche or your life, if you are not going to deal with it or, but in reality there is no danger like a bear or a giant cat who wants to swallow you.

You cannot escape from this situation, because this situation is in your own mind and you also cannot physically fight it.

Panic attacks and all of the examples stated above are not a visible and real threat (anymore), but we are programmed to fight (or flight).

What will happen?

Your consciousness will dissociate from reality and perception, because you are neither able to fight or flight.

The DPDR wants to safe you from this helpless situation, helping you with shifting the reality, to endure this ongoing threat in form of psychological stress.

Every human being will dissociate at least once in their lifetime.

Most people will not even notice it nor will they get scared by this feeling, just shaking it off and forgetting about it.

But there are severe cases of dissociation (like mine and probably yours, because you are reading this book) and if you are a very sensitive human, you will probably not be able to shake it off just like this.

It can also grow to a toxic habbit, hiding behind the dissociation when you are confronted with a stressful

situation.
Or it could be your super power, dissociating
whenever you want.
You can decide on how you would like to look at it.
I am trained like this.
If I want to, I can dissociate without being scared.
So for me it is like a kind of super power.
But, I mean, it is 2020 now, took me seven years to
get to this point.
You can get rid off it completely, though!
When all of this happened to me, there were many
things going wrong.
I was filled with self-doubt, starting another college
again with 23 years, my father and grandparents
pressured me, because they wanted me to go for a
different education.
I was really anxious about everything in my life, also
my relationship, that has just started.
I didn't want to fuck it up, that man was so precious to
me.
Due to my father's narcissism (which I know *now* but
not back then) and me being the scapegoat of the two
children he've had, I did not feel good enough for my
ex-boyfriend.
My thoughts were very toxic and I stressed myself out
all of the time, like 24/7.
And instead of the relaxing effect I wished the joint
would have had for me, it went the opposite way and
it was the trigger for all of my surpressed anxiety and

stress I have been carrying for quite some time.

It took me a while to clearly understand all of this.
There are people that never took any drugs, where the
DPDR just happened out of nowhere.
No panic attack, no drugs, no highly stressful
situation.
But the mechanism is always the same.
It could be a traumatic past experience, stress and
anxiety going on in your mind for a long time,
pressure, stress, etc. or learnt helplessness from your
childhood, where you have already mastered the
technique of using DPDR, to dissociate from
situations you are not able to bear.
Also there are people who claim that they don't have
any of the problems stated above, but the truth is:
They have.
You could just be so used to stress and anxiety, that it
seems normal to you.
We will come to this delicate topic later in this book.

*Sympathetic nervous system and the parasympathetic
nervous system*

The parasympathetic nervous system is responsible
for your inner balance and stability with the *rest-and-
digest-syndrome.*
You can see the rest-and-digest-syndrome as the
antagonist to the fight-and-flight-syndrome.

The parasympathetic nervous system plays a role in relaxing, laughing, enjoying, positivity, optimism and clear thinking.

Of course it makes sense now, that when you see a person suffering from DPDR, all of these positive aspects seem to be gone.

Lying down somewhere, reading a book, enjoying my inner peace was just impossible.

Eating food, going to sleep, watching a movie – everything was a horrible experience, nothing could give my mind the rest it so heavily needed.

If there was one little moment during my day, which I could enjoy, the anxiety and fears just destroyed it right away.

Does that sound familiar?

There even is a scientific explanation for this:

People suffering from DPDR have an overactive sympathetic nervous system.

This sympathetic nervous system is always on the lookout for danger and harm.

It is possible to cool this damn thing down if we would just activate the parasympathetic nervous system, with some little exercise step by step.

But instead, most people with this condition are feeding the anxiety with behaviour like:

- constant negative thinking about the situation they are in
- constant internet research, reading horror stories

about the DPDR
- paying attention to all of these nasty, intrusive thoughs
- sitting at home and feeling sorry for themselves, avoiding everything nice because of the anxiety and the fear kicking in

I did this, too.
And you?
If you do, don't feel caught right now, okay?
I didn't want to make you feel bad.
But I just want to put out direct and strong words, because most of the time they are neccessary, to get people out of this condition.
We allow anxiety and fear to control our lives.
This is no criticism, my only intention is to show how we are controlled by our overactive sympathetic nervous system and how fear and anxiety fuel the DPDR.

In my case, the irrational fears changed whenever one did not stress me out enough anymore.
There were some new, interesting fears my creative mind came up with.
But it was also possible for an old one to make a comeback at some point of this journey, my mind testing if it could stress me again.
And sometimes it worked.
You could even tell if you just watched me.

My body was in a crouched position all of the time, like I was on high alert 24/7.
I couldn't enjoy anything anymore.
Everything was plain and grey, there was no colour in my life to be found.
I just wanted to stay at home all of the time.
When I went shopping at the supermarket, I sometimes had to quit in the middle of the check-out process, because panic attacks appeared to happen in this situation.
That made running errands even harder.
Panic would built up even before doing anything, just because I was scared to have such a embarrasing situation in my life again.
But it is actually pretty easy to retrain our parasympathetic nervous system and to support our rest-and-digest-syndrom.
These are some of the things you can do, to silence your overactive sympathetic-nervous-system and to support the parasympathetic one:

- laugh
- smile
- walk straight up and in a „proud" position
- enjoy
- have sex
- masturbate
- cuddle with you animals or partner
- help other people or animals

- start a new project (e.g. learning a new instrument, improve your garden, things that have to be done around the house)

I know that doing these things will trigger anxiety and fear and that it seems to be impossible to do something like this right now.
A simple smile just feels so fake and weird.
It is not something that you can do just like that.
It is a step-by-step process and I want to help you with that task.
I will show you how I finally could activate my parasympathetic nervous system again.

2.3 The „nothing-helps-best" principle

As we all know, the fear and anxiety keeps the DPDR going.
There are many irrational fears and intrusive thoughts, which make it hard to enjoy anything.

Here is a little *best of* of my fears, I had to deal with:
(Please note that they could be triggers.)

- the fear of going insane
- the fear of certain people
- being afraid of my own mirror reflection
- the fear of breathing
- the fear of existing
- being concerned, that other people surrounding me could be somebody else / could be robots
- the fear of my own tongue
- being afraid of my own hands
- the fear of leaving my body just out of nowhere
- scared of the first-person-perspective (it didn't feel like my own eyes / my own sight / it didn't make sense anymore)
- afraid of losing control
- afraid of losing my own identity
- being scared of food

It doesn't matter how irrational and *crazy* those thoughts might be.

The less afraid you get of one certain fear, the crazier the next one will be.
Everything is just to give the DPDR what it needs in order to survive.
Also the DPDR and the sympahetic nervous system toy around with our eyes.
When in current danger, the sight differs from the normal one in order to see more of the upcoming dangerous situation, to have a wider angle.
The pupils are getting bigger, so it is no wonder that a lot of people affected by DPDR have issues with their sight.

A very special and utmost disturbing symptom of fears I have found during my research is, that people affected from DPDR would suddenly be afraid to have a certain kind of taste in their sexual behavior, which are very condemnable.
If you have one of these fears, let me assure you, that this is just a part of the nasty symptoms.
You are not a bad person!
On the contrary!
Most of the people with DPDR are extremely sensitive (as I said before) and empathetic.
They usually would never hurt anyone.
Please don't be too hard on yourself for those thoughts.

To get out of the chornic DPDR, one of the most

important steps is, to activate the parasympathetic
nervous system and the rest-and-digest-syndrome.
In this case we can stop the overactive sympathetic
nervous system and the 24/7 fight-and-flight-mode.
If you get your parasympathetic nervous system
enough time, it is able to reduce the level of stress
hormones (adrenaline) and you can refill your energy
tank.
And this is one of the toughtest tasks to overcome:
It needs *enough* time to do so.
Time, you were probably not able to give it, until now.
We can change things together now.
It is necessary that the toxic cycle of anxiety and fears
gets discontinued to finally cut off the supply for the
DPDR.
The way out of the DPDR needs a little bit more than
that, but it is the most important and first step to
recovery.
It is normal to fall back into old patterns in the
beginning.
It needs a lot of practice and trust to break the cycle.
But it will get easier with time.
Everytime you are *fighting* for your recovery (there
will be no real fight in that sense), you will be one
small step closer to the goal.
Also it is so important (not only regarding the DPDR),
that you will never lose the ability to laugh about
yourself.
And to practice this again, I have a ironic list for you,

of the top 10 things to do, if you **DO NOT** want to recover from DPDR:

1) Please feel pity for yourself all day long.

2.) How about searching the web again for your symptoms and the symptoms you've just had few days ago?

3.) Please just focus on your symptoms, the whole day and the whole night, try not to get a good sleep.

4.) Please lock yourself inside of your house and do not meet friends and / or do not enjoy a coffee with your family somewhere.

5.) Why not stay at home from school / work to feel like you would have an actual illness or disease?

6.) Let those irrational fears dictate your whole life and your actions.

7.) Search the web again, maybe change some keywords to find new trashy info!

8.) Continue hoping for a magical pill that will reverse everything.

9.) Lose your trust in the process because you will

have setbacks and panic attacks!

10.) Don't invest anything in you, let yourself go and don't think about doing things for you e.g. exercise, new clothes, new make up and do not invest your time in anything that could be good for you, like a new hobby.
Why don't you rather use that extra time you have, because you are just staying at home, in searching the web again for your symptoms?

Of course these top-ten-rules are exaggerated and they are not meant to hurt you in any way.
I, myself wasn't any better.
I was behaving like this for months and months!
But after a while I really got sick of this bullshit.
I wanted to get out of the DPDR so bad.
It was my primary goal in life.
And I started to only read positive recovery stories and tried to find a pattern and leaving the moaning and bad stories aside.
What was the common theme all of the blessed, recoverd people had in common?
(Leaving those aside who claimed acupuncture or vitamin B12 was their cure, we will come to that later.)
I was like a detective writing down everything on a chart and trying to figure it out.
The common theme for all of them was:

Nothing.
They did absolutely nothing.

So how should you start with the „nothing-helps-
best"-principle?
It is not as easy as it may sound.

The best way to start is to deceive yourself.
You do know that something isn't right at the moment
but you will not listen to this anymore!
Everything is okay.
And start deceiving the people around you, too.
I know, it may sound weird in the beginning.
You are not doing this to be deceptive and you are not
a liar.
You are not a bad person because of this.
You just want to help yourself and you are not lying
about anything that could harm other people!
When I started with it and irrational fears came back, I
just laughed about them in my head.
Or I even laughed out loud, which was a bit weird in
the beginning, but it helped.
It is totally fine to be sarcastic and make fun of
yourself.
„I don't care man, this is ridiculous, just leave me
alone because everything is fine."
Of course I felt like a weirdo talking to myself like
that in the begining.
But it helped.

I am free of DPDR.
If you can conquer one fear with this technique, you will notice that your subconsciousness will swap the old fear and anxiety for a new, even more terrifying thought!
With a little bit of practice you will conquer the next fear again.
„I am not interested, everything is fine, ridiculous."
That should be your mantra.
Over and over and over again.
If you need some time off to restore energy, it is really okay to stay a few days at home from work or school.
But if you can, try to lead your life as normal as it is possible.
Otherwise you will send signals to your brain, that there is something wrong and again this leads to the increase of DPDR symptoms.
I even wrote my final exams with DPDR, even though I was pondering about wether that pen was real or not.
I don't want to show you „how great" I am.
I did a lot of things wrong, really.
I just want to encourage you.
If a girl like me, totally at the bottom of her life, can make it, you can too!
During DPDR I took my first flight on a plane.
It was one of my biggest fears but at that time I didn't really give a shit about anything anymore.
I was so done with DPDR and all of the fears that I thought, I might just make that trip to England.

And I actually was proud of myself.
The first few days after my primary flight, I thought I
would not exist but the trip was great anyway.
You can do *anyhthing* with DPDR.
It is no illness, it is just your fear and anxiety that is
holding you back.
You are not handicapped in any way, DPDR is just a
feeling, not a real threat.

Now I need to talk about a uncomfortable side effect
occuring when you are on your way to recovery.
And I can assure you, unfortunately this will happen
to you as well.
The DPDR will always punish you for your bravery.
It will try to fight for you with everything available.
In fact it is just your own self trying to fight against
you.
I know it sounds schizophrenic, but to get out of the
DPDR is a scary process.
I am not going to lie about this.
But you know it now, that's why I am here to help you
prepare and to armor for the war coming.
The precious price at the end of it is gaining back your
own, wonderful life without DPDR.
But it is not an active defense strategy that will help
you win.
The trick is to not fight against it.
The waves will come in high and sometimes they
might swallow you.

It is okay to have setbacks.
Setbacks are part of the recovery.
Without a setback you don't see how far you've already come, right?
Active fighting against the DPDR will not bring you any success.
If the waves are coming, just close your eyes, lay down if you can, hold onto something, maybe a teddybear from your childhood or a lucky charm that reminds you of someone special, just hold onto it and let the waves come crashing in.
The DPDR is not a real threat and there is no harm you have to fear coming from those waves.
A key word here is *acceptance*.
It all begins with acceptance.
Acceptance, that this situation is not dangerous in any way.
Acceptance, that it is possible to reverse the DPDR.
Acceptance, that nothing will happen to you.
Letting the positive back in during DPDR is one of the scariest things I have ever felt.
If your level of fear and anxiety is high, just let them pass by like clouds on your own horizon of your mind.
There is no need to hold onto them and grab them.
You should not rate those intrusive thoughts and fears.
They are there, yes but that should be it.
That's the only reality.
You have the ability to make them into something

more meaningful, than they really are or you can just accept them for what they are.

You know now why you have them.

Because the DPDR needs all the negativity to keep itself going.

That invisible shield is fuled by anxiety and fear.

The sooner you lose the fear of the fear, the earlier you will be recovered.

But don't pressure yourself.

It takes time to get there.

Imagine you would be your own DPDR and you start feeling that your end is near.

Of course the irrational fears and anxiety will get worse, in some cases it will rise up to the extreme level.

I have went there.

And I came out without any damage.

Another advice is to dismiss everything in your life that is related to the DPDR.

I highly recommend you to not be in social media groups about the DPDR with your main account.

If you still need those groups to find comfort, it would be better to use a second account, different from your main account.

Of course my advice is to leave those groups.

But as I said, it is the little steps that will bring success.

In the end you should be gone from any group or forum on the internet.

Also put away this book (after reading of course) or any other books regarding this topic.
If you are in touch with someone who is also suffering from DPDR, my advice is unfortunately to cut off all the contact with them.
During your recovery you will notice why I am giving you this advice.
When you start recovering, you will automatically not think about this topic anymore.
It happens naturally.
If you surround yourself with DPDR in your everyday life, you are taking this possibility away from yourself.
It is the most important thing now to think of yourself.
No one else will do it for you.
It is your own responsibility to take these steps.
Creating a DPDR-free enviroment will help you tremendously.
At the beginning of my story, I have been a lot in those forums and groups on social media.
They can be helpful, but there is also a lot of toxicity.
There are people who claim that you cannot recover from DPDR, which is absolutely not true and you may even find new symptoms there for your own setlist of symptoms, because you might read something without a trigger warning.
If you are constantly reminding yourself of the DPDR on your phone or your laptop, on your bookshelf, etc., you are not giving the sympathetic nervous system a

well deserved break.

The sympathetic nervous system needs to be toned down to activate the parasympathetic nervous system and the rest-and-digest-syndrome.

This is your goal.

Don't be too hard on yourself, just go small steps and be prepared for the setbacks.

It is also good to have a person who you can really trust with your condition.

They don't have to understand it fully.

When I headed out for town, etc., I've had a few people in my life which knew that I had difficulties with being in the public.

So they knew I was suffering from panic attacks and anxiety without explaining them my weird feelings and thoughts.

It was okay for them just to know the basic stuff, so if I was gting overwhelmed, panicking or being scared in the public, I would just tell them a codeword and they instantly knew to bring me to a quiet place and hold my hand.

They didn't ask any questions and just waited with me until my attack was over.

It is a very good idea to have a few of those people in your life.

Try to explain them, that you have a condition that causes panic attacks, etc., and that you would be really happy if they could be one of your persons of trust.

Another idea is to explain your most crazy and weird thoughts to a person of trust.
In my case it was my mum.
I said:
„Mum, I know this is going to sound really crazy but with this condition, I get irrational fears and I want to talk about it with you.
You know that I am not like that usually, but I need someone to talk about these things."
So she listened and I was very serious explaining to her that I was afraid of food and atoms and, I don't know, that my whole existense and the thought of being alive just freaked me out.
Like literally everything just freaked me out at the peak of the DPDR.
I remember staring at her face, waiting for her reaction, nervous and anticipating and I was so relieved when she started laughing.
It is not like the person makes fun of you, it's just so helpful to see other peoples reaction to those fears.
It takes a bit of the seriousness away and as I said before, it is so helpful that you will never forget to laugh about yourself, too!
Being self-ironic and sarcastic is such a good remedy against DPDR.

The next step would be to find a hobby or task, that sparks a lot of joy for you.
I for myself found playing the guitar a very soothing

hobby.

I couldn't play the guitar before and so I just started learning it with the help of my ex-boyfriend and videos on the internet.

This hobby could really take my thoughts away from the DPDR for quite some time.

I didn't care about the intrusive thoughts, because I enjoyed playing the guitar so much, that I just ignored them.

Also I found myself some new crafting ideas.

Origami and crafting dreamcatcher were my new hobbies.

The whole house was full of pieces of origami and all of my friends and family had a dreamcatcher then.

This is not just to relax.

The real relaxation takes a while to come back, but this is just a simple and good idea to take the thoughts away from the DPDR and to activate your parasympathetic nervous system.

It should not be like you are looking hectically for something, the sympathetic nervous system will take this behaviour as a threat.

If you don't feel like it, you should not push yourself too hard.

It should not cause too much stress for you.

But keeping your mind busy with other things is a big help in recovery.

If you are able to focus on a book, it is quite a nice thing to do, as it can drag you totally into a new

world, that you are creating in your fantasy, with the help of the book.
So it is nice just to be in a different world for a time, taking a break from your harsh reality.
Also note that, if you are feeling happy while experiencing a new hobby or task, it could trigger some really bad episodes of DPDR.
Because the DPDR feels threatened by happiness and joy, just keep that in mind and don't fight against this feeling.
Try to accept that it is there and proceed with being happy and joyful and your new hobby.
After a while the DPDR will be silent and not disturb you anymore while doing it.
Then you will notice, that you have come a step closer to recovery.
Congrats!

Before I will end with this chapter I want to summarize all the important thoughts and steps for the „nothing-helps-best"-principle:

1. Acceptance

This is probably the most difficult, yet most important step on your road to recovery.
And what I am talking about is the *real acceptance*.
This is something you cannot learn overnight.
And being hopeless and fealing defeated by the

DPDR is not really helping with this point either.
Accepting is a process and it helps if you say to
yourself a few times a day, that you *are* accepting
your condition.
Even though you don't really believe it, it helps to say
it, because after some time, you will really feel it.
Trust the process.

2. Live your life

It is helpful that you are trying to keep your life as
normal as possible.
So if there is work or school, you should not avoid it.
It is okay to take breaks once in a while (I did need
them, too!), but you should not stay at home like you
were ill.
Having a structured everyday life will be beneficial.
Sleeping in long and just living for the moment will
not help, because there is a lot of slots and space for
the DPDR to play it's weird mindgames again.

Note from the author May 2020:
I know we are living in difficult times with the
Corona Virus all over the world.
It is also very important to keep a structured day
WITH the virus around.
I know it could be even more difficult, but maybe
you also find the time for starting a new hobby or
project and take the benefit from staying at home.

Also you could maybe help elderly neighbours, e.g.
with shopping or walking their dogs.
You will make it through Corona, I am sure of that!

Helping out people in your community, e.g. help the
elderly with their garden or keeping the community
park clean, etc., will be stimulating your
parasympathetic nervous system, as helping people
and getting the regognition for it is very beneficial for
your brain and your soul.
It is nice to have someone around who is proud of
you.
Of course you can be proud of yourself.
You are reading this book and you *want* to get out of
there.
You are here, helping yourself, learning a lot about
DPDR and yourself.
This is more than a just a small reason to be proud of
yourself.
Allow this feeling to happen.

3. Don't fight the feelings – go with the flow

This is a very difficult task as well, coming right after
the acceptance.
Fighting against panic attacks, anxiety and irrational
fears, will make the DPDR worse.
Because if your fighting against something, will send
an alarm to the sympathetic nervous system that

something is wrong.
So you'll unfortunately start the downward spiral again.
When you accept that these feelings are there, this step will be the logical consequence of the first one.
It is healthy to not judge any kind of negative thoughts or feelings appearing in your head.
I have learned a great lesson in my Yoga-class regarding this topic.
You can train your mind, too, not only your body.

Imagine yourself sitting on a wooden bench just outside of a huge paddock, the scent of bright green and lush grass inside your nose, calming you.
Inside of this paddock, there is a single horse.
It is a wild, dark, stallion, furious and strong, running and jumping.
Would you try to saddle this stallion right now trying to chase him with the great chance of getting hurt, or would you rather sit back on your bench, watch the horse, the sky, enjoy the beauty of nature and wait until the stallion was calm again?
Wouldn't you rather saddle it then?
The same goes for your mind and thoughts.
Negative, wild thoughts will come and you will not be able to tame them.
Chasing them will just use a lot of energy and there will not be a satisfying solution by the end of it.
You will just feel drained and frustrated.

*So I invite you to just sit back on your bench inside of
your mind, relax and watch the wild und furious beast
called DPDR until it is tamable again.*
Just now you will gain the control back of your mind.
Just then is the time to saddle it.

So just let it happen.
Trust is the key. Nothing bad will happen to you.
Try it out. You will survive this panic attack, anxiety
attack, wave of disgusting and irrational fears.
There is no real harm.
It will just use up precious energy to try and gain
control of it.

4. Exercise and a healthy nutrition

I have been exercising before DPDR and I always
tried hard to maintain a balanced diet.
I have read online about many ex-affected people that
state, that a balanced diet and some light exercise are
beneficial for the recovery process.
Of course a healthy and balanced lifestyle is
beneficial for the mental health overall.
It is better than having no structure, being lost in your
everyday life and drug abuse.
Also high-fat-foods and a lot of sugar can have
negative influence on the DPDR.
Fresh vegetables, lean proteins and a lot of the healthy
omega-3-fatty acids are a positive input for your body,

hormones and well-being overall.
Also reducing caffeine or cutting it off completely,
helped many of the recovered, as caffeine can induce
panic attacks and / or anxiety attacks.
I limited my caffeine input to one cup in the morning,
the rest of the day I would drink water and herbal teas.
If you are fighting with being overweight, it would be
a great opporunity to lose some of the toxic
behaviours and change them to healthy choices in
food, lifestyle etc.
But I also want to warn about extreme exercising, as I
had learned my lesson regarding this topic.
After a little break in the beginning of my DPDR
story, I went back to the gym and thought, I could
exercise like before.
Exercising increases the level of adrenaline in your
body so it can trigger panic and anxiety.
I changed to lighter sport like Nordic Walking and
swimming, even up until now.
I just realized that heavy exercising is not healthy for
me and my body and I as well can maintain my
healthy weight and health with light exercise.

5. Find people you can trust and release blocked emotions

It is always good to have a few people around you,
who you can trust with your condition.
They don't have to understand the full story and

sometimes they are just not able to understand any of this, as it is too abstract for some.

A problem shared is a problem halved.

So if you ever feel like moaning, crying or whining, it helps if you can release this together with a person you trust.

It is not healthy for this person to be a person affected by DPDR.

They probably have enough on their own plate and you could trigger each other.

A lot of people affected by DPDR are losing theirselves in the moaning, which is not beneficial at all.

You should set boundaries there!

Don't let yourself get dragged in and dragged down.

Self pitty is okay in doses, but it is the utmost important thing to get up and face the DPDR again!

6. Finding new tasks & hobbies

Looking for a new hobby forcefully, could send false signals to your sympathetic nervous system.

But finding something naturally, that you are enjoying (enjoying as much as you are able to feel) is the perfect step for your recovery.

Don't limit yourself with new ideas, e.g. „I am too old to learn …."

That is not true.

It is never too late to find a new passion!

7. Distancing yourself from the DPDR

This advice is a psychological one.
During my research, I was always reading threads
from affected that used sentences like:

„My depersonalisation causes this and that..."
„My derealisation is much worse than yours..."

I have to say that this kind of talking about the
condition is really toxic.
It is not *yours*. It's a thing that happened to you and
you will reverse it.
To make DPDR your own thing is unhealthy.
It is no illness, no disease or something like that.
Your goal would be to create a neutral distance to this
disturbance in your natural defense mechanism.
People sometimes tend to define theirselves through
the things happening to them.
And it is very common in the DPDR-community.
There are different reasons for this behaviour and I
don't want to be too judgy.
But a lot of people subconsciously enjoy the role of
the victim.
But honestly, it is time to say goodbye to the role of
the victim.
It is a toxic trait that needs professional help if it gets
too prominent in your behaviour.
The reasons for this usually lie in the childhood and

should be discussed with a psychologist.
Instead of making yourself the DPDR, try to remember the things you like about yourself.
Ask your close friends and family members what they value about your character.
You are not the DPDR!
You are your own self!

8. Avoid reading too much about the DPDR

There is a lot of trashy information going around the internet about the DPDR.
There are some shady reports about pills, that magically helped or special massage techniques etc.
Most of the time it is a cash grab.
Getting out of the DPDR and the recovery doesn't cost a thing, really.
Maybe getting some books and the things you need for your new hobby or hobbies, but that should be it.
The rest you need to recover is inside of yourself.
It is absolutely neccessary for your recovery to stop the internet research step by step.
If you still need groups on social media etc., I would advice you to create a second account to use especially for those groups.
Your normal life should be as much DPDR-free as possible.

If you are suffering from this condition from 10 years plus, I also want to implore you to consider this

method.
The longer you are dealing with this crap, the harder it seems to go away.
And it could hurt to realize that it is just that easy.
It is worth it to try it out either way.
It is never too late to turn your life around.

So it takes a discipline and courage, I'm not going to lie.
But on the other hand it is okay to be soft on yourself sometimes and allow yourself setbacks.
Guilt and shame will not help.
All of these steps helped me to gain back control over my own mind, make the DPDR disappear and I could finally feel my own emotions and self again.

2.4 Root cause analysis
Trigger warning! Just read when you are feeling stable enough!

Many people affected by DPDR are convinced, that there is something lying beneath the surface.
A lot of people consider the roots of their DPDR story in their childhood, caused by traumatic experience.
There is not enough scientific evidence that could to confirm this assumption.
I also think it could be beneficial to take a closer look.

In the English speaking DPDR-communities, they even call this condition the *coward's disease.*
I wouldn't be so harsh but there might lie a truth behind this sarcastic name.
The DPDR is a mechanism to ensure mental health during traumatic experience.
So, speaking from a logical standpoint, it makes sense that it could be learned during childhood, also called learned helplessness.
The DPDR could have a very traumatic experience in the childhood or it could be the sum of many, smaller traumatic coincidences.
Being a very sensitive human, you could already have dissociated in your childhood without really noticing it.
I think this is a very delicate topic as trauma is not easy to resolve.

What I really want to emphasize is, that this does not *have* to be the case.
But it could be.
A traumatic experience doesn't have to be an extreme one, like rape or a heavy illness.
It could be that you fell from the bike as a child and didn't receive any kisses and cuddles from your mother.
Or it could be that you were an outsider in class.

With the help of a psychologist and many therapy sessions, I found out about my traumatic past.
The family from the side of my narcissistic father abused me emotionally for decades.
This family had a toxic dynamic, just functioning by making me the scapegoat.
Just imagine all those wonderful dinners I've had there, with everyone tearing my life apart and showing my all my flaws and failures.
Cheers to that!
I did not realize this until I was digging deeper due to the DPDR.
Also, I could finally my father as someone with a narcissistic personality disorder.
I did not know this when I was a child of course, and being treated like shit by him always made me think it was my fault and that I was just not worthy or useful.

These thoughts were lying deep within my mind.

Also I found out about a physical abuse as well.
One of my caretakers in kindergarden strangled me
and hit me a few times and punished me for behaviour
that was just normal for children.

It was the most painful experience of my life.
Realizing how wrong adults treated me when I was a
kid, made my cry heavily and I remember one therapy
session, where I would just lie down on the floor and
cry like a baby the whole time.
That was my inner child, that little girl, that has been
so hurt and finally I could let it out.
Writing about this now still hurts.
But it doesn't trigger DPDR anymore.
The divorce of my parents in the early years of my life
probably was traumatic as well, looking back to it
now it was the best decision my mother could make.
Living with this person called my father would have
destroyed me.
Being his daughter was never enough for my father.
He praised my sister and she was the golden child.
It was not her fault and she had her own difficulties as
the golden child, which were different from mine but
it had negative effects on her, too.
My father once said to my face, that I will never show
up in his family tree, if he'd ever create one on paper.
Like I was non-existent.
Rings a bell?
I was feeling non-existent a lot during DPDR.

My grandmother always used to force me to call him, even though I tried to explain her that I did not want this.

I always had to work double or triple hard to get acknowledgment from this side of the family, if I got it in the end.

Most of the time they just didn't recognize or acknoweledge my good traits or success in any form.

My mother was my angel, because of her I am sane and stable and a grown, proud woman.

When I was with my mum, I could be the way I wanted to be, she gave me the feeling I am enough and that she loved me.

No matter what, I have always had her support.

So she prevented a lot of consequences without even knowing it.

Of course I told her everything about what happened there when I was with this side of the family.

But words like narcissistic personality disorder and such were not common in the 90's.

People have so much more knowledge nowadays. There was a lot of self-doubt going on within me.

Looking back now, I would say that the root for the DPDR was set back then, my early childhood and when I was a young teenager.

Children are often the victims of their parents own unresolved trauma.

They don't know how to distance themselves or

defend themselves from maltreatment, so they often dissociate instead.
This is what you call learned helplessness.

The next point is to take a close look at your social circle.
There is a kind of humang beings, which I call the *soul vampires.*
Everybody knows at least one soul vampire.
These people are just talking about themselves, using your good will without giving back, pity themselves all day long and they make you think that they are the poorest people on the planet.
And also they want you to think they are so kind and selfless.
Those people are not really interested in you, but they have a good sense whenever you raise a suspicion what they really are and they suddenly will be the kindest and most supporting person that you know.
But just long enough to get you back on their hook again.
They *can* be people with a full blown narcissistic personality disorder, but they don't have to be.
Not everonye is a narcissist but many people with those traits have a very developed narcissistic side in their personality.
Most of the time you will feel drained when you are with those people.
They always say that they will help you out, but if you

really need them, they are not there.
Most of the time these people are just a lot of talk and no action.
If you have extreme soul vampires in your social circle like I've had, they can also leave you empty and destroyed once they don't need you anymore.
It is possible that your mother, father, sister, brother, partner, grandparent, uncle, best friend, boss, co-worker is one of those soul vampires.
A lot of people suffering from DPDR do have at least one of those surrounding them.
Most of the time people with this condition are selfless, caring, kind and empathetic.
We are magnets for soul vampires.
A lot of times we have problems with setting our own boundaries and people are taking advantage of this fact.
It took me a while to realize, that setting healthy boundaries and protect them is my own responsibility.
Most of the humans do not care because what they are most about is their own good.
If someone goes too far, you have to tell them.
If someone crosses a line, you have to tell them.
If someone is treating you like shit, you have to tell them.
And if they don't accept the fact that you are cultivating and nursing your borders, maybe it is time to let these people go.
I said it once, I will say it twice.

If someone loves / likes you, they will accept your personal space and boundaries in the end.
There is a nice exercise I have learned from my psychologist.

In the beginning it felt really wrong to do it.
I was used to speak up for myself, but my boundaries and walls were tore down in an instant by my toxic family.
So I was never used to someone who would respect them and respect me.
But love also means respect.
And to safe up my energy, I just stopped saying „no" if someone was invading my space.
I just let it happen, because I couldn't see a way out of this.
If you speak up for yourself, a toxic circle around you will call you „mad, crazy, arrogant, narcissistic, not very feminine (if you are a woman), ridiculous" etc.
Watch the people around you, watch them closely.
See who is respecting you and who isn't.
Notice it and if you have to, drop this person.
Start pondering wether the relationship with this person is balanced or not.
It is for your own good.
Back to this exercise.
I did this exercise with my ex-boyfriend many times, it got better everytime.

Exercise: Setting boundaries

Sit yourself down on the ground with a person you trust.
Take a long piece of yarn und create a circle around you.
This is your visible boundary.
Look your person into their eyes and tell them:
„This is my boundary.
You and nobody else has the right to invade my space.
I will not let you set foot beyond this border.
This is my home.
Nobody is allowed in without my own permission."

You are visualizing your boundaries.
This is such an empowering and strong exercise.
I felt so bad doing this for the first time, I was crouching because I was expecting punishment for setting my boundaries, something I unfortunately was used to due to my childhood.
Also it helps you to bring your boundaries to your consciousness.

A lot of times during my research, I have read from people that one of their parent treated them not very well.
Egoists, sociopaths, narcissists, psychopaths, etc. are toxic for their children.
Often there is a trigger which reminds us of our

childhood, but because we want to push those nasty memories aside, the DPDR steps in to protect us.

In most of the cases, where the child was sexually abused, the DPDR is not able to safe the child's soul anymore and in many cases, the time victims of sexual abuse develope mental illnesses like psychosis, multiple personality disorder, schizophrenia and so on.

I was very scared due to the DPDR, that I thought I maybe was a victim of sexual child abuse.

But most of the time you will surely have flashbacks when sexually abused as a child.

Said in different words: You will definately know it, sooner or later it will come out.

As long as you are just scared of being a victim, you normally aren't one.

Obsessive compulsive disorders can also be a reason for the DPDR.

Also the compulsion to control everything is often connected with DPDR.

There are cases of DPDR where it seems, that there is no reason to be found in the past.

Of course this is possible, too.

An extreme level of stress over a certain period of time and / or a panic attack induced by drugs or not or just severe anxiety can be the root of the DPDR, without having past childhood traumas.

I think it is always a good idea to take a look beneath
the surface, to see if something lies there.
To solve these issues are not just beneficial for the
DPDR-situation, it is beneficial for your whole life.
To me it is important that I didn't take these steps
without professional help.
In Europe therapy sessions are covered by national
health service most of the time.
If you are not able to afford a therapy session, maybe
find services that can help you for free.
Also seeking help in your chruch etc. could be an idea
for this task.

2.5 Medication and mental clinic

There is not one pill on the market, that can take the DPDR away.
I know there is research done at the moment, but it actually doesn't need that magical pill.

I have heard of a few people affected by DPDR, that have had success with different antidepressants.
If you think about it logicially, it makes sense of course.
Antidepressants are drugs that should help to relieve anxiety, fears and negative thoughts.
If the effect starts to kick in, the sympathetic nervous system will cool down and finally it can take a break.
I have also been using antidepressants duing my life.
Not for DPDR but for depression that came a few years after the DPDR-episode in my life.
They helped me quite a lot and I felt more „clear" in my head.
I am off off these now, but I would take them again.
In the end this choice is up to you.
Of course those drugs have side effects like weight gain, weight loss, heart issues, nausea, etc.
Also the blood should be checked with samples on a regular basis, because those drugs can have affects on your organs.
In my opinion antidepressants could help you in the beginning to let go of the DPDR.

Weaning them off could trigger a massive setback, weaning antidepressants off is not a fun thing to do in general.
This is my experience speaking.
So you should consider the positive and negative effects of those drugs.
They will not take the DPDR away, but they can support you.
If you are interested in antidepressants, you should talk to your psychiatrist for professional advice, as some side effects could trigger DPDR symptoms, like a increased heart rate.
During the DPDR-episode in my life, I took natural capsules with lavender to calm myself.
Also there are some natural sleeping aids like valerian.
To help with the brain fog I took natural fish oil capsules with a lot of omega-3-fatty-acids.
There are some positive reports about the fish oil capsules to be found amongst the recovered.

I also want to talk about a stay in a mental clinic.
When I first wrote the book, I kind of was biased because I have heard a lot of horror stories coming from people who have claimed they went to a mental clinic in order to get help with DPDR.
They told me they got the wrong diagnosis just after one therapy session, got medication they didn't want to take etc. etc.

Since I've had a major depression last year, I now know better because I admitted myself to a mental hospital due to this depression.

And to be honest, I really liked it there.

I didn't *need* to take any medicine, I just wanted to try out antidepressants and the doctors there helped me a lot.

Also I've had therapy sessions, yoga, nordic walking, creative therapy and music therapy.

When therapy was over for the day, I was free to go outside and have a walk, go to the city center, meet friends for a coffee, etc.

I just had to be back before the last check by the staff for the night, and that was when the doors of the clinic would be locked until the next morning.

I have also met a patient there, who actually was currently suffering from DPDR at that time.

Of course I could help him a lot.

He also said the clinic was beneficial for his health, mostly because he was too exhausted to take care of his life.

It was a welcomed break for him.

So I have two thoughts about this:

- First, the signal to your sympathetic nervous system could be „danger" again.

So it could trigger more depression, anxiety and overall DPDR symptoms if you admit yourself to a mental hospital / clinic.

- Second, I do think it could be helpful for some people affected by DPDR.
Especially when you are just at the end of your energy level and overwhelmed by everything.
If you need a break from home it could be an ideal place for you.

You should not expect therapist to talk about DPDR.
They know about this condition, but it is no real mental illness for them either.
So you could be surprised that the therapist is not listening to your DPDR symptoms, really.
They know that DPDR is anxiety-based and full of irrational fears and panic.
My therapist never really spoke about my symptoms with me, because in the end it is actually the same, over and over again.
It is counterproductive.

If you are aware of that and realize that your symptoms are not important for a successful therapy and if you need to take a break from your life, a clinic could be just the right thing for you.
As long as you don't feel bad about, I don't see negative impacts of a stay in a mental clinic.
When it sends positive signals to your brain, it can be more than beneficial for you.
It is important to make the DPDR not the main focus in the clinic, otherwise you won't get out of it anytime

soon.

When admitting yourself to a mental clinic or hospital is absolutely a horrible idea for you, like it was for me back when I dealt with DPDR, it is not a good idea to go there, as it would signal „danger" to your sympathetic nervous system.

This is really about personal preference.

I can just talk about the very positive expierence I've had in one, not for DPDR but for depression and I would do it again.

I was able to just relax there and try out the medication without any fear or anxiety, because there was always a doctor and psychologist around who could help go through negative episodes and side-effects.

2.6 Panic attacks

There is a lot of very helpful information about panic attacks on the internet.
But I also want to give my two cents to this topic, as panic attacks often appear while having DPDR.
I've suffered from some severe panic attacks during the beginning of my DPDR-story but as soon as I found out about the physical mechanics behind them, they were not a big deal anymore at all in my case.

As I said many times before, people suffering from DPDR have an overactive sympathetic nervous system, which is responsible for a constant fight-or-flight-syndrome.
That means, your body thinks constantly it is under attack or there are any dangers, that means it will have a physical effect sooner or later, as you are producing a high amount of adrenaline.
The adrenaline is needed for either the flight or the fight.
But where does all of this adrenaline go, when there is no real danger?
That's right: During reduction of the adrenaline in your body, there will be a panic attack.
You could also exchange the negative word „panic attack" for the word „energy excess".
An increased heart rate, breathing rate and pulse rate, problems with inhalation and a shaking body are the

consequence of a high level of adrenaline, amongst some other symptoms.

These are all a natural response of your body to the excess of adrenaline.

If you are getting scared now because of this feeling, your sympathetic nervous system kicks back in again and even MORE adrenaline will be produced from your adrenal gland.

The more you get scared of a panic attack (that you have because of high levels of adrenaline), *the more adrenaline will be produced.*

There is no real danger that has to be dealt with, so the body is looking for another way to get rid of the excess adrenaline.

When you are getting scared by the initial panic attack, the second one will follow and so on, and so on, and so on.

The way out of panic attacks sounds very easy but also needs a little bit of practice.

You basically need to break the cycle.

The first and a very important step is to look back to your history of panic attacks.

- When do they appear? (While driving the car etc.)
- How is my own reaction to a panic attack? (Am I reacting with more anxiety and panic?)
- Is there a pattern behind it?

Sometimes it seems that the panic attacks appear randomly, but in fact the subconsciousness and your memory of anxiety is working in the background.

Let me state a example.
I had the most severe panic attacks always during my grocery shopping trips.
The initial one started somewhat early during the DPDR.
I probably was pretty freaked out about something during grocery shopping (remember? I was totally scared of food and eating food!), I cannot remember the exact reason, though.
It happened: I couldn't breathe, my heart was beating like crazy and I thought I would faint or die.
I dropped everything in my hands and ran out of the supermarket, people staring at me.
I sat down and prepared to die but nothing happened.
But I was too ashamed to go back inside and instead I went home and ordered food.
My brain saved this horrible memory.
Everytime I would do the grocery shopping I was afraid of having a panic attack again.
I was afraid of this horrible situation and the embarrassment.
Other people probably never found it embarrassing, but it is usually the way you feel when you have panic attacks.
So I was already in a very scared and anxious mode

before I even stepped inside the supermarket.
My body was already in a high alert mode, so
adrenaline started to build up in this moment already.
I even had a panic attack during check-out and just
ran off.
I watched my body and my physical reactions closely
during shopping, every second I thought it would
happen again.
And of course it happened again.
So my anxious mind already connected one bad
experience to the act of grocery shopping, my
subconsciousness kicking in when I had to go to the
supermarket again, my body was on hight alert →
producing adrenaline and the next panic attack came.
For me it was the same situation with commuting to
work every morning.
I did have a uncomfortable situation on the bus in the
beginning of my DPDR-story and I developed this
anxious feeling taking the bus in the mornings and
evenings.
I've had many panic attacks on my bus trips.
I couldn't escape and run away from the bus.
That's when I have learnt about the best way to deal
with panic attacks, beause I was basically trapped.
As we can clearly see, reacting with irrational
decisions like running out from the supermarket, etc.,
or reacting with even more anxiety and panic, we are
putting fuel into the fire.
The trick is to not stimulate the sympathetic nervous

system even more.

The best way to do this is to simply let the panic attack wash over you.

I know it might not be *that* simple in the beginning. It would be best if you could try this out in a place, where you feel safe.

So if a panic attack is knocking on your door at your home for example, just sit down and try to let it wash over you.

It is contrary to the feeling your body is giving you, which is trying to escape from this situation.

So it takes a little bit of training and will power.

But this is actually the best and easiest way to deal with panic attacks, as panic attacks are just a physical side effect of the excess adrenaline your body produced with no real danger in sight.

Whenever you can, sit down und just let it happen. The less anxiety and stress you will put into them nasty attacks, the sooner you will get out of it.

Due to my biological education, I was easily able to look behind the mechanics of the attacks, so I got rid of them in a very short amount of time.

Also it is very helpful to shift your focus from your body more to the outside world.

Do not judge every little weird heartbeat or shaking you might notice.

I wish you good luck with defeating the panic attacks!

2.7 Intrusive thoughts

The DPDR and panic attacks are enough to deal with already, but there is also a symptom called intrusive thoughts giving the affected a hard time.

In my case the intrusive thoughts were absolutely dreadful and I had a hard time handling them.
I alredy had them before the DPDR but with this new condition, I totally lost control of them.
They really can feel like hell on earth and they have drained a lot of energy from me.

Intrusive thoughts are, of course, not positive most of the time – on the contrary: They are absolutely dreadful and the most horrible thoughts you are able to think of (a logical consequence, as the DPDR needs fear and anxiety to keep itself alive).
Existential thoughts are a part of this in most cases, too, as they can be quite scary, because the answer to them is not known by any human really.

It is possible, that thoughts of extreme violence and / or violent sexual and disturbing practices can manifest inside of your mind.
The thoughts can get more extreme everytime you will lose the fear of one certain thought, as the DPDR needs your anxiety and fear to exist.

Let's check some facts together.
Just two percent of the sum of all the thoughts
counted in 24 hours are positive thoughts for a person
without any mental issue or disorder.
About one quarter of the sum of all of the thoughts
counted in 24 hours are destructive thoughts and 70
percent are subconscious and non-important thoughts,
which just pass without bringing the attention to them.

Let's now take these facts and transfer them to a
person affected by DPDR.
It is completely logical that most of the destructive
thoughts and non-important ones, which you normally
wouldn't care about, are now the most important
thoughts to shift your focus on.
They manifest as intrusive thoughts and compulsive
thinking because they offer the most delicate fear and
anxiety for the DPDR to stay present.

Let us try to go back together to the time before the
DPDR hit you for a moment.
I am sure that you have thought about the existense of
the universe, humankind, animals, food etc. before
and it of course kind of gave you a weird feeling,
because fact is we don't have answers to those
questions, but it didn't scare the shit out of you!
All of us think about God, religion, universe, life after
death, reality, time etc. without having anxiety attacks

People without DPDR or anxiety-based-disorders just accept the reality for what it is.

They also accept that there are no real answers to those questions (yet).

Remember when I talked about that wild stallion in your mind before and how to deal with it, this is a perfect training for this issue.

Sometimes I felt so defeated, like I have just fought a war on my mind and I lost it.

In the beginning I continuously tried to control *what* I was thinking.

But it's not possible.

No matter if you have mental issues or not.

Nobody can control their thoughts for longer.

There is subconscious thinking which cannot be controlled, no matter what.

With the DPDR in order you will shift your focus to terrible, ugly and dreadful thoughts, which are pure horror.

Those thoughts were the worst symptom for me and I tried so hard to gain back control of my mind by fighting them hard to go away.

There are people in the DPDR community that state, that those intrusive thoughts are used by some people to not have to think about a past trauma.

Instead they cannot let go of those irrational fears and intrusive thoughts.

I don't know if this is the case for you.

In my case it was not.

It was just something that produced the most fear and anxiety and the DPDR loved to tortue me with the most horrible thoughts my mind could possibly come up with.
It was like a 24/7 gore movie up there.

How did I get rid of them in the end?

The good thing is, I don't have them anymore.
I have found out that it is the most important step to not identify yourself with those thoughts.
As I discussed before, it is totally normal to have all kinds of thoughts, if they are pervert, disturbing or violent or peaceful.
It happens naturally and is out of our control.
The thoughts you have are not part of your personality.
You are not a bad person because of them.
The compulsive thinking and intrusive thoughts really triggered a fear of my own self.
„What kind of human am I, to have those thoughts?".
The guilty feeling was very present inside of me.
But having around 60.000 thoughts a day, it would be wrong to identify yourself with them.
It is your own right to have thoughts of whatever kind.
Just thinking about to murder someone, doesn't make you a murderer.
Similar to defeating panic attacks and irrational fears it is key, that the intrusive thoughts are going to lose

their power over you.
The more disturbing a thought is for you, the more likely it is that it will manifest itself als a compulsive thought.
A thought you just can't ever stop pondering about.

There is another step you can take to lose them.
It is like a higher, advanced level and it will take some guts.
It is not only about to have a „ I don't care" attitude.
It is more about challenging them.
Yes, I know I always say something like „don't start the fight, because you will lose it anyway" and it is true!
But with those nasty, intrusive thoughts there is another possibility.
It is a method I call the *desensitilization.*
I tried to provoke a loss of control with this method.
Let's take one of my top ten intrusive thoughts, which triggered a lot of fear:

„I am not real. The world is not real. Everything isn't real."

I have always had the fear that acknowledging this thought, would somehow trigger either the end of my life, the end of my sanity or the end of the world and I tried to avoid the thought with all of my energy.
How did I proceed, then?

I was just fed up with all of this and I faced it.
I challenged it.

„Oh yeah?
Okay. I am not real.
You are right.
And now?
The world is not real.
We don't exist.
The world doesn't exist.
And now?"
Nothing happened The world kept turning.
The reality was still the same.
I didn't snap.
Everything was just fine.
And I just let my thought exist in my mind.
I didn't fight it to be gone anymore.
I just proved myself that my intrusive thoughts don't
have any power at all.

Another example.

„I am going crazy now. I will lose it. I will snap. "

And so I thought:

„Okay.
I am giving away the control now.
Let's snap, brain!

Let's go crazy.
I cannot do this anymore.
If I am ought to go crazy, let's do it now.
I don't mind anymore.
Do what you want."

And nothing happened.
I didn't „go crazy" and I am more sane than ever.
And even if...?
What *really* **is** the worst case that could happen?
Is it reversible?
Of course it is. Most of the things in life are
reversible.

With this method I have found relief very quickly.
With challenging the intrusive thoughts and no
negative outcome of this, they lost their power over
me.
It doesn't matter what we *believe.*
The reality won't change because of our thoughts.
We don't have this kind of power.
What I liked to say to myself about this is:
„It doesn't matter if I believe if that street light is real
or not. If I walk towards it, it will hurt me in the end
anyway."
The world keeps turning, with you believing in it, or
not.
It would be wise to not waste your time in those
thoughts and feeding the fears anymore.

Here are some of the most popular intrusive thoughts while having DPDR:

The intrusive thought of...
- ... going crazy
- ... killing someone you love
- ... believing the world is not real
- ... having a pervert side
- ... losing your identity
- ... commiting suicide without having control of it
- ... believing you are already dead and just dreaming
- ... losing the grip on reality
- ... not going to survive the DPDR
- ... believing the world will end soon
- ... doubting the existense of humankind

3. At the end
3.1 Medical aspects

Sometimes, in very rare cases, the DPDR roots in physical causes.

Some of them could be:

- physical damage to your brain
- epilepsy
- hormonal issues
- autoimmune disease (Hashimoto Thyroiditis e.g.)
- deficiency of micronutrients

Micronutrients, especially vitamin B12 is helpful with the DPDR, as it has positive effects on the nervous system.
You should not supplement vitamins without having a blood test beforehand.
It is probably not the „remedy" for the DPDR, but it can support you while healing from it.
As I said, those reasons are very rare, but for some people maybe a possibility to think about.

3.2 More advice and last words

So this is already the last chapter in this book.
It was a pleasure for me to write down this
information for you.
I could help many people with my story and my tips
and advice.
There was a lot of positive feedback over the years,
one woman actually went to Australia (!) for her year
as an au pair, even with DPDR because this book was
so empowering for her.
All of my advice in this book is written with all of my
heart and with my bestest intentions and knowledge.
I am free from DPDR for over 5 years now and it
never came back even once.
There are a few more tips, that helped me on my
journey to recovery.

1. Autogenous training / ASMR videos
That was a good help when I could not sleep or when
my anxiety level was too high on my daily commute
on the bus.
You should not start with autogenous training when
you are in the middle of a panic attack.
It could send false signals to your sympathetic
nervous system.

2. Green tea / herbal teas
During the day I drank a few cups of green tea (watch
the caffeine!) and herbal tea in the evening.
Tea is very helpful to restore the inner balance and it

was always a lovely break that could give me at least five minutes of rest.

3. Sex, tenderness, kisses, masturbation
All of these things are a perfect stimulation for the parasympathetic nervous system, which shoud be your primary goal (next to calm the sympathetic nervous system at the same time).
Maybe the last thing you want to think about now is sex or masturbation.
It was the same for me.
I couldn't do it for months.
But then I researched all the things helping in stimulating the parasympathetic nervous system and I started masturbating again.
The first orgasm with DPDR was nothing less but amazing.
So many feelings at the same time! Wow!
Then the sex with my (ex-) partner followed.
The first time we did it with DPDR, I started crying because he transported so many emotions while having sex, I finally *felt* again, even if it was just a little bit.
If you have a partner and your sex-life is like non-existent, just tell him that you carefully want to try to exchange sinful tenderness between the two of you.
You can always stop when it is too much for you at the moment.
It is also a really good habbit to be gentle with

yourself.
Also meant in the sense of not being harsh with
yourself, when you think you failed or that you are not
strong enough at the moment to proceed with any of
the steps written about in this book.
You will not be strong enough on some days.
It is okay to have a shitty setback-day and start over
again.
You don't want to have stress or harshness in your life
at the moment.
Be as gentle, calm and positive as you can!

4. Don't look back
After a while you will start to notice how you
positively changed over the time.
If you notice this, try not to think about the time when
you were miserable, until you are really stable.
(Like I am now, writing this book).

5. Acupuncture, physiotherapy & massage
It can ease the physical tension and it will activate
your parasympathetic nervous system.

6. Treat yourself
Maybe there is something material in your life, that
you always wanted to get.
Or maybe you could use a day at the spa?
If you can, go treat yourself.
This will stimulate your parasympathetic nervous

system.

7. Just smile
This is a very simple trick.
Try to smile as much as you can.
It probably will feel weird in the beginning, but it is a positive signal for your parasympathetic nervous system.
I watched funny cat videos to help me with smiling.
After a while I even started laughing.
It was such a beautiful experience to be able to laugh again and really feel it.
This is like a exercise and you will have to conquer some fears and anxiety for it.
I started with smiling at myself in the mirror reflection every morning, which was a hard task for me.
As you maybe remember, I hated to look at myself in the mirror or on photographs.
But I just wanted to really get rid of the DPDR, so I faced myself and started to smile.
It got better with time.

8. Reading
Reading fantasy novels is such a good possibility to escape to a different world for a time and give your mind a well deserved rest.
It was hard for me to focus on the book in the beginning, but it got better over time.
You should avoid reading stuff about the DPDR and if

you can, start to leave social media groups and / or internet boards as soon as possible.

s

9. The excessive moaning

Not to be judgy, but it seems that one of the favourite hobbies for people affected by DPDR is practicing self-pitty and moaning.

It is okay to break down once in a while, it really is.
I did that.
I was lying on the floor like a little child, kicking and screaming in frustration.
I remember destroying a piece of art on a canvas I just created right before my nervous breakdown, because I could not feel it.
I was not able to feel this painting and my emotions when I looked at it, but I wanted to so badly, so I just destroyed it.
And then I cried because I could feel anger again.
I was so happy.
I did moan, and I wallowed myself in my mental mud.
But it is necessary to stop yourself before it gets to excessive.
Because this toxic trait will not bring you any further.
It will just delay your recovery.
Let it out once in a while.
Cry like a baby once in a while.
Be frustrated like a little 4-year-old kid not getting his beloved candy, once in a while.
But also never give up and start again after a

breakdown or a setback.
Also don't define yourself with the DPDR.
„My DPDR"
„My Trauma"
„My DP"
„My DR"
„My dissociative disorder"
This is toxic.
It is not yours. It is a thing that happened to you, it's not your fault.
Rather use:
„The DPDR I am dealing with right now."
„The trauma I unfortunately had to experience."
It seems like a small step, but it will help a lot to distance yourself from this condition.

10. Grounding methods
These grounding methods are helpful especially with strong symptoms of derealisation.
Some people affected have the symptom, that their body is not really existent anymore and they feel like they would just be made of their eyes.
To put small stones in your shoes will help you to „ground" yourself.
Another method is to tell yourself what you are doing at the moment, like a storyteller reading a novel.
„I am walking to the bus stop right now to take the bus to work. I am on the bus now and I am listening to music."

This helps to adapt to the reality to your mind.
Different kind of meditation is also very helpful to practice not giving attention to the intrusive thoughts and irrational fears you are dealing with.
You can focus on a certain object in your room, e.g. a vase.
While focusing, you will have many thoughts running through your mind.
Important here is to not validate or rate these thoughts.
Just let them pass by.

Last words

With this book, I am able to give you the techniques and advice you were looking for to recover from DPDR.

There is always a individual set of symptoms, but the way to recovery is always the same, as the mechanism is always the same.

The key to gain back your life lies within you.

This condition is harmless, but it doesn't feel like it.

In the end, it's just a *feeling*.

Start with small steps.

One thing after another.

Don't put too much on you in the beginning.

Setbacks are normal.

Setbacks are healthy.

Setbacks are okay.

Setbacks will help you see how far you've come.

You will come out of a setback.

It is as sure as death and taxes.

The DPDR will get sronger, the more you are healing.

Setbacks will be hard.

But they will lose their power after some time.

Read this book again if you need more motivation.

If you can, go and travel.

See new places.

It is just a *feeling*.

Don't let a feeling dictate your life!

Don't let fears dictate your life!

It is the only one you have.

You will get it back.

I know it.
I could do it.
I was so deep and lost in this miserable condition.
I thought I would die.
I thought I would go insane.
I thought I would end up in the mental hospital (which
is not that bad at all!) or on the gaveyard as a corpse.
I was afraid of thinking my mum is posessed by a
demon.
I was afraid of thinking my ex-boyfriend wanted to
kill me.
I was skin and bones because I was afraid of food.
I was afraid of my own body.
Everything I took for granted was taken away from
me.
Reality seemed off.
Be thankful for all the beauty that lies within being a
human and our wonderful planet.
Be modest and thankful for all of your friends and
family, that will try to understand you as good as
possible.
Take your strength and courage back and show that
feeling what you are really made of.
Be thankful for the little things in life.
Be thankful, that you don't have serious illness like
cancer etc.
Find a person you can trust and laugh about your
irrational fears together.
When they want to punish you for that, say

„Fuck off now, I am having a great time!"
Try to act normal and even if you don't feel like it:
Fake it 'til you make it.
Maybe set some new goals for your life.
A new job?
A project for the community?
Maybe you want to write a book about your
experience or a fantasy novel?
Why are you not starting with it?
Don't hesitate because of a *feeling*.
Be patient.
It will all work out in the end.
I know it.
Maybe I am a person who thinks, that the glass is
always half full.
Maybe I am.
But you can be that person, too.
Be creative, brave and wild.
Let yourself be inspired by other recovery stories.
Believe those veterans.
They have been through this shit.
Face those intrusive thoughts – you will notice that
they are not able to do any harm.
Try to be a good human.
Try not to be filled with bitterness.
Treat yourself.
You deserve it.
Try to work on your past hurt and traumas.
It will help you not only with the DPDR, it will help

you to lead a more positive life overall.
Try out some new things.
Stimulate that parasympathetic nervous system as much as you can.
Enjoy everything.
The sun, the air, dogs, the food, movies, your time and friends.
You only have this life.
And at last you have this one.
No matter how hard it is at the moment, having this life is a gift.
Expand your mind.
Try to see the DPDR as positive as possible.
It will change you for the better.
Be humble.
Be kind.
Be friendly.
Be yourself.
Because nothing can change that.
Your identity, your feelings, your emotions – all of this is yours, no one can take this away from you.
It is all just hidden and covered by the DPDR.
It will come back to the surface, piece by piece.
Why are you not smiling?
Who took that beautiful smile of yours?
There is no reason not to smile.
There is no reason to be afraid.
You are not alone.
Remember: We are many.

And I am here with you.
I believe in you.
You will make it. I know it.

With the best wishes and lots of love,
Always thinking of you lost ones,
Your shattered selves,
Like I have been once
I was so deep and lost in my own
Shattered self
That I thought I could never be one again
But I could make it
I thought the worst thoughts
I feared the worst fears
I endured the strongest panic attacks
I was convinced I could not make it out.
But I did
Because we are beautiful souls
Who just lost ourselves a bit
In this gruesome world full of ugliness
But the world needs a beautiful soul like you
To have some beauty shining through the darkness
Your soul will be whole again very soon

Sincerely yours

Vanessa

Printed in Great Britain
by Amazon

18335761R10073